21 DAYS

OF

INNER-HEALING

FOR

THE SOUL

Dr. Bonnie B. Hill

He Restoreth My Soul

ACKNOWLEDGEMENTS

This book was written to bring healing to the body, soul and spirit. It is designed to provoke your thinking, cause you to examine where you are now, and give you the power to change for the better.

The need for Inner Healing is universal; although many deny it, the fact is, it is a reality. We all have a place to work from, work through and work towards.

I have watched so many lives changed through the ministry of Inner-Healing for Women, and I am grateful the Lord called me to this deliverance ministry because it has healed me as well.

First, I want to thank my parents, the late Elder John Robinson., Jr. and Mother Maxine Robinson for believing in me when God called me to Inner–Healing.

I'm thankful to my husband, Clem. Thank you for your patience and love, even when you didn't understand the late nights, or, helping others make it through the night, taking strangers in and comforting them, and hiding battered wives. Baby, thank you for believing in me and for your support throughout the years.

I want to acknowledge my children, who are my first ministry and my first Inner-Healing assignments (even though you're grown, you're still my assignments.) I thank you all for sharing me and allowing me to serve throughout the world.

I'd like to thank the hundreds of men and women who trusted me with their lives for the past 25 years of this ministry. To every Pastor and church, in every city and state, that has allowed the ministry of Inner-Healing to operate within your facility, thank you. To every sorority that has allowed me to bring the ministry to your group, thank you. To Restoration House and Francis Watson, thank you for bringing your court-ordered women to Inner-Healing and allowing me to be a part of their "start-over". I am eternally grateful to everyone who has not only prayed for this ministry, but sown seed toward its furtherance.

To my spiritual daughter who pushed this book out, Pastor Jefferida Hines-Doggett. I am so grateful for your persistence and consistency. It would still be on the tablet in the closet, but you said, "We are going to do this", and we did!! Thank you.

Dr. Bonnie Hill

DEDICATION

I would like to dedicate this book to my dad who left behind footprints of grace. Daddy, you will never be forgotten. To my mom who has always been there for me, and, my sisters, Sharon and Janice who fit in wherever I need them too. To my daughter, Crystal who keeps me straight and keeps the bottom line, the bottom line, and my granddaughters who are my gems; Mandy, Megan, Mariah, Mahogany, Aniya, Kalis, and the angel of them all, Kinslee.

FORWARD

The perplexities and complexities of life can leave one with both internal wounds and external limitations. Out of the miry pressures and circumstances that we sometimes find ourselves inflicted by, we must ascribe to a heavenly download to help us heal from our earthly dilemmas and dysfunctions. THE PURSUIT OF HEALING STARTS WITH SEEKING THE COUNSEL OF GOD.

God's counsel guides you so you can come through any situation you're facing in victory. Nothing is more precious than receiving the counsel of the Lord. That counsel holds the treasures of wisdom, peace, joy and prosperity we need to walk in the fullness of God's healing and blessings.

If you are a believer, the Counselor Himself—Holy Spirit—lives in your spirit to lead and guide you. However, you have to draw out the deep waters of His counsel, as Proverbs 20:5 says: "Counsel in the heart of man is like water in a deep well, but a man of understanding draws it out" (The Amplified Bible). You draw it out by giving God your attention as you spend time in His Word and in prayer.

If you are too busy to fellowship with God in the Word and prayer, then all the hubbub and clamor of daily life can make it difficult to hear Holy Spirit's counsel. To draw that counsel out, you must get intentionally quiet in your spirit, silence external distractions, and listen attentively to Him.

Another key verse related to drawing out Holy Spirit's counsel is Proverbs 20:27: "The spirit of man [that factor in human personality which proceeds immediately from God] is the lamp of the Lord, searching all his innermost parts."

The King James Version calls the spirit of man "the candle of the Lord." It is in your spirit that you receive God's light of revelation. Revelation is essential to healing because it has the ability to rearrange your reality.

Now, this natural world is ruled by darkness. In it we find the lower ways and thoughts of this earthly life. However, God's higher ways and thoughts reside within the deep well of your spirit. They must be drawn out so you can receive God's understanding and wisdom. That's what the psalmist meant when he said, "You cause my lamp to be lighted and to shine; the Lord my God illumines my darkness" (Ps. 18:28, The Amplified Bible).

When you have a decision to make and you don't know what to do, God will enlighten your darkness. His counsel guides you in the way of wisdom so you can come through the situation you're facing in victory.

Holy Spirit lights our candle with His revelation. He illuminates our darkness with the wisdom of God, "once hidden [from the human understanding] and now revealed to us by God" (1 Cor. 2:7).

With God's counsel, we can walk in victory when there is turmoil around us. We can be like the children of Israel, who had light shining in their homes when darkness lay on the land of Goshen so thick that no one moved for three days (see Ex. 10:21-23).

In the same way, the light of God's counsel can shine out of our spirits into a dark and confused world. We aren't limited by what is going on in the natural realm. We can draw out the counsel of God and walk in His higher ways.

In order to take hold of the high life, we must first let go of the low life. We can't hold on to sin and enter into God's realm of light, glory and victory. Sin desensitizes us so we can't hear what God is clearly speaking to us.

In addition, the cares of this world, deceitfulness of riches, and lust for other things can enter into our hearts and choke out the Word (see Mark 4:19). We must fling aside weights and sins and take hold of God's counsel. The less cluttered our hearts, the more sensitive we are to hear God and walking in His higher life—a life of liberty, healing, deliverance and abundance.

As we draw upon God's counsel from within, He can order our steps. We can walk in the good things He has planned for us. "The steps of a good man are ordered by the Lord: and he delights in his way" (Ps. 37:23, NKJV).

So, when you face a situation and don't know what to do, confess, "God lights my candle and enlightens my darkness!" Spend time in the Word and prayer. And expect God to give you divine counsel and order your steps as He heals you.

Make the decision to let go of the low life of the world. Walk in the light and take hold of the high life of God!

The following 21-Day Devotional, penned by the incomparable Kingdom Practitioner and Mother in Zion, Dr. Bonnie Hill, is encased with the heart and mind of God to release, reinforce, and reconcile the reader into the stability that comes from being *healed from the inside out.* It is by God's counsel has Hill developed this manuscript to impart truths that will maximize the spiritual capacity of the reader into a whole, happy, and holy condition and position. As you read BE HEALED; as you digest BE MADE WHOLE; as you live it out PROSPER...

Ricardo D. Weaver, Sr., DD, CLC, CPT

R. D. WEAVER MINISTRIES

www.rdweaversr.com

Table of Contents

INTRODUCTION

Genesis 2:7, "And the Lord God formed man of the dust of the ground, and breathed into his nostrils the breath of life; and man became a living soul."

The word "soul" in this instance comes from the Hebrew word "nephesh" which means:

- That which breathes, the breathing substance or being
- The inner being of man
- Seat of emotions and passions
- Activity of the will, mind, character, appetite and desire.

Apart from the breath (the ruach, wind or spirit) of God, man was a lifeless form, but when God breathed into his nostrils, everything that He had placed within him became alive. Man's will, emotions, passions and desires were now alive.

Also locked within the man was the woman who had not yet been made. But here's the awesomeness of God; though woman had not yet been made, when

God breathed life into man, he also breathed life into the woman so she came forth, from the womb of man with living emotions, wills, desires and passions.

But, as was experienced by the first family, the soul of man can become overwhelmed, inundated and even devastated by the circumstances of life. However, as the psalmist says in Psalms 61:2, "*From the end of the earth will I cry unto thee, when my heart is overwhelmed lead me to the rock that is higher than I.*" The word "heart" in this verse is from the Hebrew "*leb*" which means mind, inner man, seat of emotions or passions, soul, thinking or memory. In other words, when my thinking is overwhelmed, my memory is overwhelmed, my emotions are overwhelmed lead to the Rock that's higher than I.

In this 21-day journey of the Inner Healing for your soul, may you be reminded that Jesus is the Rock of your salvation and it is in His name alone that you, the righteous, can run into and find safety. May you find complete restoration, renewal and healing for your mind, body and spirit.

MY PERSONAL DESIRE

My daily desire is to be changed in my heart, mind, and spirit. And, since I know that I am saved, am being saved and will be saved, I want my inward parts without contamination so that I may embrace whatever God is doing and/or wants me to do when I awake.

I yearn to be so in-tune with Him that I will know immediately when I am off beat. As Apostle Paul said in Philippians 3:10 (KJV), "*That I may **know him**, and the power of His resurrection, and the fellowship of His sufferings, being made conformable unto His death.*"

My heart's desire is for spiritual insight, a daily soul revival, a zeal for the lost and to gain discipline from the things suffered along life's journey.

I'm amazed at how God works to fulfill both His will and His purpose through His children.

Lord, help me to do your will, today and every day. In Jesus' name, I pray. AMEN!

MY DAILY PRAYER

Father, in the name of Jesus; I take authority over this day, and pull down every negative force or energy that is planning to operate against me today.

I call forth the Spirit of favor, counsel, might and power to fall upon me, in Jesus' name.

I shall excel this day, and will possess the gates of mine enemies. My ears shall hear good news and my future is secure, in Jesus' name.

The anointing of God is upon me and gives me favor in the eyes of God and man all the days of my life.

There will be no poverty or lack in my body, soul or spirit, and, I receive now the anointing and the wisdom which my adversaries are not able to resist, in Jesus' name.

Lord, cause my heart to rest and trust in You, in the name of Jesus, I pray. Amen!

DAY 1

"GREAT IS HIS FAITHFULNESS"

> *It is of the LORD's mercies that we are not consumed, because his compassions fail not. They are new every morning: great is thy faithfulness.*
> Lamentations 3:22-23 KJV

God's faithfulness simply means He is reliable, unfailing, can be trusted, and is thorough in performing His duties.

Great is Thy faithfulness," O God my Father,
There is no shadow of turning with Thee;
Thou changest not, Thy compassions, they fail not
As Thou hast been Thou forever wilt be.

"Great is Thy faithfulness!" "Great is Thy faithfulness!"
Morning by morning new mercies I see;
All I have needed Thy hand hath provided—
"Great is Thy faithfulness," Lord, unto me!

We often speak of His greatness, yet, because of the limitations in our human language, we inadequately describe Him. We say "awesome", yet He's greater! We say "magnificent", yet He's greater! We say "supreme", yet He's greater!

Psalms 104:1-5 (KJV): *Bless the Lord, O my soul. O Lord my God, thou art very great; thou art clothed with honour and majesty. Who coverest thyself with light as with a garment: who stretchest out the heavens like a curtain: Who layeth the beams of his chambers in the waters: who maketh the clouds his chariot: who walketh upon the wings of the wind: Who maketh his angels spirits; his ministers a flaming fire: Who laid the foundations of the earth, that it should not be removed forever.*

Reminiscing upon the faithfulness and greatness of God in our individual lives will invoke an attitude of gratitude. We are grateful when we remember the ways that He has made, the times He's shown His mighty hand to bring us up out of a hard place. Have you ever been sick and He healed you? Or avoided an accident that you know should have happened? Have you ever lost a job, yet He still provided? How do you explain it, other than to say, it was a supernatural move of God?

Great is the LORD, and greatly to be praised in the city of our God, in the mountain of his holiness. Psalms 48:1

Today, focus on His greatness, and allow it to remind you of how great you can become in Him.

Even in your weakness, His strength is made perfect. His greatness gives you grace to win every one of life's battles, challenges, obstacles and pressures. You will conquer them all because He is your strength and you can do all things through Him. His grace gives you the ability to do what you could not naturally do on your own.

In King David's time of strength and weakness, he could speak with confidence that *"The LORD is my light and my salvation; whom shall I fear? the LORD is the strength of my life; of whom shall I be afraid?"* Psalms 27:1

Oh, to know the greatness of God and His strength!

So, no matter what you face today, allow God's greatness to strengthen you for the task. Always remember that His grace is sufficient for your weight.

PRAYER: Lord, please help me trust you with everything in my life today. Show me your greatness, in Jesus' name. AMEN!

AFFIRMATION: Today I will rest in His faithfulness; faithful is His name and He will not fail me. (repeat 3 times by faith)

DAY 2

"GOD IS OUR SOURCE OF STRENGTH"

> *Seek the Lord and His Strength, seek His face continually.* 1 Chronicles 16:11

Finding strength in life's greatest difficulties can seem impossible, however, what may seem impossible with man is possible with God. Matthew 19:26 *"But Jesus beheld them, and said unto them, With men this is impossible; but with God all things are possible."* Jeremiah 32:27 *"Behold, I am the LORD, the God of all flesh: is there anything too hard for me?"*

His divine strength keeps, protects and sustains us. The safety of His arms gives us refuge from the storms and trials of life, and courage and faith to move forward.

Unfortunately, we cannot avoid life's valley lows and moments of discouragement; it's just a part of it. However, when we learn to completely submit to God's will and His way, we can endure hardness as a good soldier, without losing our peace and joy, knowing He will work all things out for our good.

Please allow me to testify: There has been countless times in my life where I needed the Lord to give me strength to not give up under life's pressures. He did! As I recount, I can't even imagine what my results would have been, had I acted in my own strength and on my own accord. God proved Himself to be a very present help in the time of trouble, and, since He is no respecter of persons, He will do the same for you. Indulge me as I tailor Psalms 124 to my life:

*If it had not been the Lord who was on **MY** side, now may I say;*

*If it had not been the Lord who was on **MY** side, when men rose up against **ME**:*

*Then they had swallowed **ME** up quick, when their wrath was kindled against **ME**:*

*Then the waters had overwhelmed **ME**, the stream had gone over **MY** soul:*

*Then the proud waters had gone over **MY** soul.*

*Blessed be the Lord, who hath not given **ME** as a prey to their teeth.*

***MY** soul is escaped as a bird out of the snare of the fowlers: the snare is broken, and **I AM** escaped.*

***MY** help is in the name of the Lord, who made heaven and earth.*

Never run away when you don't feel the strength to endure. Stand still and trust God with all your heart, and don't lean to your own understanding. God is not a man that He should lie, therefore, He will bring you through whatever storm you face because He has promised to never leave nor forsake you.

Temptations, tests, trials, heartaches, heartbreaks, criticisms and struggles will make you feel as if you can't go on, but you must do as David did, and encourage yourself in the Lord YOUR God. Tell yourself, "Yes, I can! I can go on! I can endure! I can maintain! I can hold out! I can stand because *'Greater is He that is in me than he that is in the world'*."

Trust God in your times of need; rely on Him and you will discover that divine strength will arise in the moment you need it most to overcome any situation. Today your tragedies can be transformed into triumphs through the strength that God is releasing upon you through the person of Jesus Christ.

You have the strength to survive, the power to endure and the ability to overcome. Your responsibility is to trust God, listen to His voice, and then obey His commands. And, may you find comfort in knowing that you are not alone in your trials, neither are you without strength.

There is no greater expression of trust in God than to say, "Father, I can't do this on my own, but I know with Your strength I am able to overcome all things."

Hymn-writer, Charles Wesley said it best when he penned these words:

"Father, I stretch my hands to thee, no other help I know. If thou withdraw thyself from me, ah, whither shall I go?" (Public Domain)

PRAYER: Father, thank You for giving me the strength that I need for today; in Jesus' name. AMEN!

AFFIRMATION: I have the strength of the Lord and am well able to overcome. (repeat 3 times by faith.)

DAY 3

"I SHALL NOT BE MOVED"

> *I have set the Lord always before me: because He is at my right hand, I shall not be moved.* Psalms 16:8

As women, we are moved by our emotions and many of our decisions are birthed out of our personal needs and for selfish reasons. However, we must remember, emotional decisions are dangerous.

Nonetheless, whenever you have a personal need from the Lord, it is not selfish to say Father, "I" need thee. The word "I" in this instance implies that you are individually determined to get whatever you need from the Lord.

King David is one of my most favorite Bible characters because, despite his challenges, trials and troubles, he experienced great fellowship with the Lord. It was in the presence of the Lord where he received instructions, directions, counsel, discipline and chastening. His fellowship with God gave him assurance that even if he walked through the valley of the shadow of death, he didn't have to fear, because the Lord was with him; His rod and staff comforted him, and He even prepared a table before David right in the presence of his enemies.

Fellowship with God is imperative, otherwise, how will you know with assurance that He is at your right hand, your advocate or your defender? Isaiah 41:10, *"Fear thou not; for I am with thee: be not dismayed; for I am thy God: I will strengthen thee; yea, I will uphold thee with the right hand of my righteousness."*

Consider the promises made to you this day: I will strengthen you and will uphold you with my right hand!! If God said it, that settles it; He will do just what He said!

There are so many benefits in God's right hand, however, they will only be personally realized if you walk in His statutes and obey His commands. You must live a life that is pleasing to Him. With the Lord as your guide, there is no trouble or trial that will defeat you. You are victorious in Him!

Esther, a woman of great faith and courage, found herself in a dilemma where she had to make a decision for her own life as well as the life of her nation. Although she was afraid and stated the words *"If I perish, I perish"*, God gave her the strength she needed, and her courage saved an entire nation.

Here is what we can glean from this story: Our obstacles may seem insurmountable, overwhelming, impossible and impassable, yet, if we are steadfast, unmovable and always abounding in the work of the Lord, victory will be our portion. If we are spiritually grounded and not driven and tossed by the winds of life, we will triumph over every situation and in every circumstance.

"Now thanks be unto God, which always causeth us to triumph in Christ!"   **2 Corinthians 2:14**

Set the Lord before you, so with much assurance you will know that He alone will uphold you, He alone will sustain you, He alone will bear you up, and you will not be moved because you're firmly rooted and grounded in Him. Keep your eyes on Him and say, as the psalmist did in Psalms 121:1-2, "*I will lift up mine eyes unto the hills, from whence cometh my help. My help cometh from the LORD, which made heaven and earth.*"

PRAYER: Lord, help me to be still and know that you are God. Help me to walk in the full assurance of faith today, in Jesus' name. AMEN!

AFFIRMATION: I affirm today that I shall not be moved by what I see or hear, nor by the trials that will come my way, because my eyes are set on You, my Savior and Lord.

DAY 4

"YOU CAN TRUST HIM IN THE STORM"

He maketh the storm a calm, so that the waves thereof are still. Then are they glad because they be quiet; so he bringeth them into their desired haven. Psalms 107:29-30

And he saith unto them, Why are ye fearful, O ye of little faith? Then He arose, and rebuked the winds and the sea; and there was a great calm. Matthew 8:26

Regardless of how strong we are, there are some things that we can neither avoid nor escape, therefore, we need the strength and the peace of God to endure. While everyone seeks calmness and the peace that surpasses all understanding, what we must realize and know is that a calm, or state of tranquility, usually comes AFTER rough activity. It is what you experience AFTER turbulence, AFTER turmoil, AFTER conflict, AFTER confusion, AFTER the storm.

The good news is, not only did Jesus leave us His peace as he ascended into heaven, but he continues to give peace to those who trust Him with their daily storms.

Storms can be very dangerous, as well as cleansing. Storms can kill as well as cause things to live again. Some storms may last an hour, while others last for days, however, each storm has a purpose. If you live long enough, you will experience a storm, and storms are not prejudiced; they effect the rich and the poor, the saved and the unsaved, the old and the young, the just and the unjust. But, what a blessing to know that when a storm is out of our human control, it is under God's divine control because HE STILL STILLS STORMS!!

The storm is in His hand; the extent of the storm is in His hand; He created the storm therefore he can demand it to cease when it has served its purpose.

Fire, and hail; snow, and vapors; stormy wind fulfilling His word. Psalms 148:8

And they feared exceedingly, and said one to another, "What manner of man is this, that even the wind and the sea obey Him?" Mark 4:41

Let your storm serve its purpose because, when it is over, you will experience a release of serenity and healing to your mind, body and spirit. Always remember, the sun will shine again! The late Reverend Timothy Wright wrote an old song which says, *"I'm so glad troubles don't last always...weeping may endure for a night; keep the faith, it will be alright. Troubles don't last always!*

Calmness comes to you today! Take three (3) deep breaths and as you slowly exhale, focus on the peace that He gives to you today.

PRAYER: Father, I acknowledge that my storm is in your hand and that it must serve its purpose for my life. But, I know that whenever you say "peace" there will be peace. Help me to patiently wait on You so that I may experience the peace and serenity that only You can give, in Jesus' name. AMEN!

AFFIRMATION: Today I will ride the waves of life, because I trust the one who can speak to them and they obey.

While riding through the storm,

Jesus holds me in His arms,

I'm safe!

DAY 5

<u>"IT WILL WORK FOR YOU"</u>

> *And we know that all things work together for good to them that love God, to them who are the called according to His purpose.* Romans 8:28

(Paraphrased) And now we know, to them that love God, all things work for good.

Gospel artist, Dottie Peoples sang a song some years ago titled He Meant It for My Good. Because of God's sovereignty and supremacy, the things that the devil meant for evil God can and will use them to work out His perfect intent for our lives. But, we must be persuaded that He knows the thoughts that He thinks toward us, and that they are thoughts of good, not evil, to give us an expected end. Philippians 2:13 says *"For it is God which worketh in you both to will and to do of His good pleasure."*

As stated in day 2, trouble is a part of life. According to Job 14:1 *"Man that is born of a woman is of few days and full of trouble."* The good news is that if you allow trouble to run its course, your troubles can become treasures. In other words, you can benefit, richly, from what you walk through. The Bible says in Psalms 34:19 *"Many are the afflictions of the righteous: but the Lord delivereth him out of them all.* And then, Psalms 119:71 says *"It is good for me that I have been afflicted; that I might learn thy statutes."*

Although it does not feel good, there is strength in knowing that our light affliction (these trials and tribulations, hurts and pains, disappointments, persecutions, distresses, rejection, oppressions, etc.), which is but for a moment, worketh (continually) for us a far more exceeding and eternal weight of glory. In other words, it benefits us because God's purpose is being worked out in us, through us and for us. We must not focus on what we can see, but on what we cannot see, for, what we can see is temporal, but what we cannot see is eternal!

In my book titled Memoirs, I exposed much of what I went through to become who I am today; teenage pregnancy, drugs, rebellion, rejection and other struggles, but, God had a plan for my life. Looking back causes me to say, "Thank You, Lord" because, in the midst of everything, the good, the bad, and the ugly, the Lord proved Himself to be my present help in trouble. He loved me in-spite of me.

Today, regardless of what your situation looks like, feels like, or is, constantly remind yourself that He's working it out for your good!! Don't ask why, just praise Him despite what your natural senses tell you. Cast all your cares on Him, because He cares for you, and *"Be careful (anxious) for nothing; but in everything by prayer and supplication with thanksgiving let your requests be made known unto God."*

PRAYER: Father, today I submit my will to Yours, and even if I don't understand, I will trust you. Make me to know your will; in Jesus' name. AMEN!

AFFIRMATION: Whatever I face today will be working for my good and for His glory.

DAY 6

"ACCEPTING THE PROCESS"

> *Not that I speak in respect of want: for I have learned, in whatsoever state I am, therewith to be content.* Philippians 4:11
>
> *Better is little with the fear of the Lord than great treasure and trouble therewith.* Proverbs 15:16

I believe that one of the biggest problems humanity has is a lack of contentment.

The International Standard Bible Encyclopedia describes contentment as the ability "To be free from care because of satisfaction with what is already one's own." Contentment in Hebrew means simply "to be pleased." The Greek meaning brings out the full force of the word in 1 Timothy 6:6-8 *"But godliness with contentment is great gain. For we brought nothing into this world, and it is certain we can carry nothing out. And having food and raiment let us be therewith content."* Hebrews 13:5 says *"Let your conversation be without covetousness; and be content with such things as ye have: for He hath said, I will never leave thee, nor forsake thee".*

As women, we must be careful to practice discipline in every area of our lives, because a lack thereof can be very costly in the end. Oftentimes, what we want most, and can't seemingly live without, will bring about the most stress upon us. If you are a person who lives to impress others or who constantly seeks the validation, affirmation, approval and/or acceptance of others, you're bringing upon yourself undo stress and pressure. You will live beyond your means and buy what you cannot afford for the sake of impressing others, and your own pride can drive you to despair.

A valuable lesson to learn is this: Who you are is who are, and, all you can do is all you can do. Don't live your life trying to make an impression on others because, at the end of the day, you'll be the only one struggling to figure out how to get out of what you've gotten yourself into. Ultimately, you're not living for yourself but for others, and, the one(s) you're trying to impress are more than likely also trying to impress. So, the question becomes: Who am I when there is no one to impress? Sometimes the process of becoming, achieving, excelling, accomplishing or succeeding may take a little longer than expected, but accept the process, because it is in the fullness of time, or in your due season that you can truly reap your harvest.

A friend once told me that she could not afford to take a day off from work because of the responsibility of paying for things she'd bought but could not enjoy. She had bought new chairs but was either too tired or didn't have time to sit in them. Our conversation caused me to examine my own life and the reason for some of the things I'd acquired. Does it really matter how much I paid for my house, my car, my shoes or clothes? If I am on the verge of losing it all, will the people I've lived to impress help me keep it or will it be a conversation piece? If I become sick from the stress to impress, will they even come to visit or even pray for me? It is imperative, my sister, that we take care of ourselves, and, if we want to last, we must make the necessary changes, starting with letting go of the need to impress others.

According to the Mayo Clinic, "Indeed stress symptoms can affect your body, your thoughts and feelings, and your behavior. Being able to recognize common stress symptoms can give you a jump on managing them. Stress that is left unchecked can contribute to many health problems, such as high blood pressure, heart disease, obesity and diabetes."

The reality of life is this: sometimes a job you've served for years suddenly closes, loved ones die, marital statuses change to divorced or widowed and, in many instances, your income drops from two to one. In other words, life itself is stressful, but to couple it with the need to impress others only adds unnecessary, uncalled-for, pointless, needless and useless stress.

Your peace of mind is what's most important, for, what good is it to have a big house but no home, a huge bed but no sleep, a fancy car that you struggle to keep each month, someone in the house with you, yet you're still alone? Our peace must mean more to us than the things we possess. Luke 12:15b says, "*for a man's life consisteth not in the abundance of the things which he possesseth.*" Contentment is a hard lesson, but is one worth learning.

The Apostle Paul said, "*I have learned, in whatever state I'm in, to be content.*" Whether we have enough, not enough, just enough, or more than enough we must learn to be content. Jehovah Jireh is our provider and He will supply all our needs according to His riches in glory. Stop stressing, and trust God!

PRAYER: Father, today I need your help. Show me how to de-stress from worry. I don't want to live prone to heart attacks and strokes, so, help me to live with inner peace and rest in my soul knowing that in whatever state I'm in you've got me, and all is well, in Jesus' name. AMEN!

AFFIRMATION: I affirm that I will accept where I am and embrace where I am going from here.

DAY 7

"HOW LONG HAS IT BEEN FOR YOU?" That's Long Enough!

> *"And a certain woman, which had an issue of blood twelve years, and had suffered many things of many physicians, and had spent all that she had, and was nothing bettered, but rather grew worse, when she had heard of Jesus, came in the press behind, and touched his garment. For she said, If I may touch but his clothes, I shall be whole. And straightway the fountain of her blood was dried up; and she felt in her body that she was healed of that plague."* Mark 5:25-29

Today, we will consider a woman who is only known to us by her issue or condition. This woman dealt with a flowing issue of blood for 12 long years. Leviticus 17:11 tells us *"For the life of the flesh is in the blood."* Blood is fundamental to the function of every cell of every component in our bodies, and if there is not enough, your bodily functions deteriorate and you die. This woman had bled constantly for 12 years, and despite the doctors' attempts, nothing was helping. As a matter of fact, she grew worse. She was in desperate need of a miracle.

When she heard of Jesus, she had to make a quick decision. Now, it's not written in Scripture, but I can only imagine how the enemy played with her mind to cause her to question whether she could receive the healing she so desperately needed. Jesus always had a multitude of people thronging him, so, to get close to him wasn't an easy feat, however, this woman was determined to make the rest of her years the best of her years. I can imagine her saying, "I can allow this thing to kill me or push me into my new level of life!"

To receive her healing would take every ounce of effort, energy and strength she could muster up, but she pressed! She pressed to get up out of bed! She pressed to put on clothes! She pressed to face a people that had ridiculed and ostracized her, especially those who held onto the Mosaic law in Leviticus 15:19-20 which says *"And if a woman have an issue, and her issue in her flesh be blood, she shall be put apart seven days: and whosoever toucheth her shall be unclean until the even. And every thing that she lieth upon in her separation shall be unclean: every thing also that she sitteth upon shall be unclean."*

After getting to where Jesus was, the press continued because, she knew it wasn't enough to just be in His vicinity and it wasn't enough to just throng Him; she needed to touch Him. This no-named woman said within herself *"If I may but touch His clothes* (or the hem of His garment) *I shall be whole."*

So, my sister, how long has it been for you? How many years have you been stuck in the same place with the same condition, the same issue, the same situation, the same affliction? How many years have people known your symptoms but not your problem?

I, like many of you reading this book, can relate to this woman because of my own issues. I not only suffered from my past but I was suffering in my present; suffering from a broken heart and a wounded spirit. Leading and bleeding; broken but still praising. And I rejoice today because Jesus Christ, my healer and deliverer, came my way, and just like that woman, I made a decision to not let Him pass me by so with every ounce of my energy, I touched Him.

I was tired of the way my life was heading; tired of fixing my face but my heart was broken; tired of trying to "fake it til I make it". I was desperate because I didn't just want to be healed; I wanted to be made whole. So, I prayed for the Lord to fix me on the inside so it could manifest on the outside.

Are you the woman with the issue? Have you been dealing with it for years, trying to hide it because of the embarrassment or shame? Are you emotionally bleeding? Spiritually bleeding? Relationally bleeding? Physically bleeding? Financially bleeding? Can you muster up enough strength to reach out one more time? Press into His presence, touch Him with the desperation of your heart and you will be made whole.

Pick yourself up out of this place of defeat and press into your place of victory! No, it won't be easy, but it will be worth it! Desperation always brings restoration! This woman's desperation pushed her into Inner-Healing. She pressed with the expectation of being whole. What is your expectation? Faith without works is dead!

Today you must decide that you will not die like this! Jesus said, "*I've come that you might have life, and life more abundantly*." Decide today that you will live and not die, and you will declare the works of the Lord. If you touch Jesus, He will touch you back. Don't stop until you reach Him!

PRAYER: Father God, your daughter needs you…Heal me, mend me, restore me in Jesus' name. From this day forward my issues become my victories. AMEN!

AFFIRMATION: I will do my part and take responsibility for my Inner-Healing by first owning my emotional and mental state. I will go toward Jesus the healer of my soul. He restores me. (Say this 3 times)

"Reach out and touch the Lord

As He goes by;

You will find He's not too busy

To hear your heart's cry;

He is passing by this moment

Your needs He will supply;

So, reach out and touch the Lord

As He goes by."

(Public Domain)

DAY 8

"YOU WILL GET THROUGH IT!"

> *Thus saith the Lord, the God of David thy father, I have heard thy prayer, I have seen thy tears: behold, I will heal thee.* 2 Kings 20:5

Knowing the will of God for your life is imperative if you are going to walk in agreement with Him. The Scripture makes it abundantly clear that God regards our relationship with Him above everything else. He commands us to love Him with all our heart, soul and mind, and, to seek His Kingdom first and everything else will be added.

When you truly know God, then you have assurance that it is His will and desire that you are healed and made whole; spirit, soul and body. The Hebrew word for heal is "rapha" which means to make thoroughly whole. In Matthew 8:2-3, there was a leper who came to Jesus and worshiped Him saying *"if thou wilt, thou canst make me clean. And Jesus put forth His hand, and touched him, saying, I will; be thou clean."* In other words, Jesus said to him, "It is my desire that you be cleansed."

Sometimes healings happen instantly, and, the Scriptures point to this fact: Matthew 8:3, "*And **immediately** his leprosy was cleansed.*"; Mark 2:12, "*And **immediately** he arose, took up his bed, and went forth before them all; insomuch that they were all amazed, and glorified God, saying, 'We never saw it on this fashion'.*"; Mark 5:29, "*And **straightway** the fountain of her blood was dried up; and she felt in her body that she was healed of that plague.*"

At other times healings take place in stages or a process, and the Scriptures also point to this fact. Mark 8:23-25 says "*And He took the blind man by the hand, and led him out of the town; and when He had spit on his eyes, and put his hands upon him, He asked him if he saw ought. And he looked up, and said, **I see men as trees**; walking. After that **He put his hands AGAIN upon his eyes**, and made him look up: and he was restored, and saw every man clearly.*" Also, in Luke 17:12-14 it reads, "*And as he entered into a certain village, there met him ten men that were lepers, which stood afar off: And they lifted up their voices and said, Jesus, Master, have mercy on us. And when He saw them, he said unto them, 'Go shew yourselves unto the priests'. And it came to pass, that, **as they went**, they were cleansed.*"

So, on this eighth day of your journey toward Inner-Healing for your soul, I believe it is befitting that we deal with the process of healing. It is easy to rejoice when a miraculous healing takes place, or, whenever you experience a "suddenly" But, how do you handle it when, instead of a "suddenly" you have to deal with a "gradually"?

The Oxford Dictionaries define process as a series of actions or steps taken to achieve a particular end.

Process will always have pressure, but pressure will always have purpose! The process of healing was never intended to be easy, but thorough; and to rush the process can literally cause a setback. When a woman has major surgery, i.e.: a hysterectomy, she's told by her doctor that the healing process will take 6-8 weeks. During that time, she is not to drive, lift anything heavy, do any strenuous cleaning or even return to work. Before the 6-8 week deadline is accomplished, she will start to feel better, and oftentimes will return to her normal activities, not considering the fact that her inward parts are still healing. God doesn't want you to just feel better; He wants you healed and made whole!

Each of us will experience brokenness at some point in our lives; emotional, physical, relational, financial, spiritual, etc. But how else could we effectively testify of God's healing power if we've never experienced it?

During this process of Inner-Healing, it is vitally important that suppressed and hurtful memories be dealt with. Suppression is a coping mechanism and is defined as a conscious form of repression. You choose to not engage or talk about distressing feelings or thoughts. You are aware of them and are not overly intimidated by them, but just decide to put off dealing with them for a while.

I'd like to share with you some very interesting information found in an online article on Fitlife.tv posted on August 24, 2015 by Doris Dahdouh titled "This Is What Happens To Your Body When You Suppress Your Emotions". To read the full article, you'll need to go to this link: http://fitlife.tv/this-is-what-happens-to-your-body-when-you-suppress-your-emotions-original.

- *Suppressing Emotions Can Cause Stress.*
- *Suppressing Your Emotions Can Cause Serious Mental Illness.*
- *Suppressing emotions denies the brain the freedom to work properly and efficiently.*
- *Suppressing Emotions Can Cause Weight Gain.*
- *Suppressing Emotions Can Cause Serious Physical Illness. You become more vulnerable to diseases and disorders when under continuous pressure.*
- *Suppressing Emotions Can Affect Gut Health.*

> *Honesty with yourself and others is imperative in obtaining your healing.*

Twenty-three years ago, the Lord gave me the ministry of Inner-Healing for Women, and I immediately found out that I couldn't just "do" ministry; I had to be processed for it; I had to be the first partaker. Several things began to happen to shake up my life, and, whereas I thought it was persecution, I later found out it was preparation. (Did you catch that?) In ignorance, I was praying against the will of God because I was operating out of a place of scattered emotions. Let me suggest to you to never allow your present feelings to determine your destiny; frustration can form or shape your future.

For the ministry of Inner-Healing to be effective, I had to allow God to deal with the part of me that others couldn't see. The Lord said to me, "If I can't touch you, then you can't touch them." So, I had to deal with things I'd suppressed for years and it caused an overwhelming sense of mixed emotions. Uprooting suppressed thoughts, feelings and emotions caused me to pray and cry many days but I found out that it was thrusting me into my healing. In other words, it was working for my good!

Sometimes to obtain your healing, it's necessary to write down your feelings and emotions, however, the negative side to that is, you will have to allow yourself to feel the pain. This causes many women to give up because it seems easier to just ignore reality, dismiss the hurt, or act as if it doesn't bother you. Listen, life presents moments where you're not alright, and it's okay to not be okay momentarily, however, you must determine that you will not live in that state.

Be encouraged, and know that if God brought me through He will bring you through as well, for, He is no respecter of persons. Don't be afraid to call out to Him, and pray with the confidence that He hears your cry. Psalms 34:15 says *"The eyes of the Lord are upon the righteous, and His ears are open to their cry."*

Not only does He hear your cry, but He sees your tears. Psalms 56:8 (NLT) says *"You keep track of all my sorrows. You have collected all my tears in your bottle. You have recorded each one in your book."*

Daughter of Zion, God wants to heal your every hurt and disappointment; He wants to take away all your guilt and shame, your oppression and depression. You may be able to hide your wounds from others, but the all-seeing eye of God knows exactly where you're hurting the most and He is the Balm of Gilead, ready and willing to bring you to complete healing, restoration and wholeness.

No matter how broken or wounded you are, the word of the Lord for you today is *"For I will restore health unto thee, and I will heal thee of thy wounds, saith the LORD (*Jeremiah 30:17*).* Be healed in Jesus' name, and know with assurance, YOU WILL GET THROUGH IT!!

PRAYER: Father, thank You for being a present help in the time of trouble. I know you hear my cry and I am grateful. Regardless to what I face, I know that I will get through it because You have promised to never leave nor forsake me, and I trust Your word. In Jesus' name. AMEN!

AFFIRMATION: I am healed, I am being healed and I will be healed in every area of my life.

DAY 9

"DON'T LOSE COURAGE"

> *"But you, be strong and do not lose courage."* 2 Chronicles 15:7 NASB)

Courage; the quality of mind or spirit that enables a person to face difficulty, danger, pain, opposition, challenges of life, etc., with fearlessness, bravery, calmness and firmness. Courage (Hebrew) is chazaq which means "to strengthen, prevail, harden, be strong, become strong, be courageous, be firm, grow firm, be resolute. Courage is not the absence of fear, but it's acting despite fear. It is feeling fear and moving forward anyway. To lose courage is to become despondent, discouraged, discarded, or dispirited.

David had a giant several times his size and weight but he didn't allow fear of the giant's threats to stop him. He was so confident in the "name of the Lord" and God's ability to give him the victory, that he armed himself with five smooth stones and a slingshot, and defeated the greatest thing that had ever stood before him.

Courage causes you to conquer your fears, and, *God has not given us the spirit of fear, but of love, power and a sound mind* (2 Timothy 1:7). Fear, according to 1 John 4:18, has torment, and the torment of fear will paralyze you and prevent you from moving forward.

Time after time we've missed the move of God for our lives because of the lack of courage. This lack has hindered and prevented us from reaching our fullest potential, being all God has designed, and attaining everything He has for us.

When fear of rejection, loneliness, criticism or even failure has its grip on you, you'll spend your life circling the same mountain, aimlessly wandering and drifting like a ship without a sail. And, the key to breaking free is courage!

In Numbers 13, the Israelites were faced with a situation of obtaining or remaining. God had shown them His hand time and time again. He'd parted the Red Sea, led them through the wilderness, gave them His law, led them through the desert and got them to the edge of their promise and then told Moses to select twelve men to go spy out the land and bring back a report. Please note: God already knew what was in the land, but it did not change His promise. Please also note: they were at the edge of obtaining the promise. The spies came back with the evidence that the land was fruitful, the cities were fortified, the people were strong BUT the children of Anak, in other words, giants were in the land.

Numbers 13:30-33

30 And Caleb stilled the people before Moses, and said, Let us go up at once, and possess it; for we are well able to overcome it.

31 But the men that went up with him said, We be not able to go up against the people; for they are stronger than we.

32 And they brought up an evil report of the land which they had searched unto the children of Israel, saying, 'The land, through which we have gone to search it, is a land that eateth up the inhabitants thereof; and all the people that we saw in it are men of a great stature.

33 And there we saw the giants, the sons of Anak, which come of the giants: and we were in our own sight as grasshoppers, and so we were in their sight.'

Caleb was the man with the courage because he declared that they were WELL ABLE to possess the land. Regardless of the giants or anything that would oppose them, God had promised them the land of Canaan, so, all they had to do was go get their inheritance! The spies who had lost their courage said:

- We can't do it

- The people are stronger than us

- They will devour us

- We look like grasshoppers in our own eyes.

It is amazing how quickly they had forgotten the things God had brought them through already. They forgot His promise and that He's not a man that He should lie; they only focused on their abilities or inabilities. They allowed the negativity of the majority to determine their decisions which were ruled by a lack of courage.

Fear and the loss of courage will cause you to be held captive in relationships that are not healthy. You tolerate physical, mental and even verbal abuse because you, like ten of the twelve spies, see "them" as stronger than you.

Courage is what you need to take control of your life. I once had a friend who was in a terrible relationship and was being abused in every sense of the word. She lacked the courage to walk away, and died at the hands of the one who said, "I love you". Fear locked her in, bound and held her as its prisoner.

Another friend was being raped by her husband but lacked the courage to disclose it for fear of his threatening's. His role in the church was more important than her role as a wife, so she continued to live in fear.

These ladies are a small representation of the many women who either feel they cannot survive on their own, or who is married to a preacher, deacon or community leader and care more about protecting his reputation than her life. The problem is, we're passing these insecurities onto our daughters and their low self-esteem will cause them to never face their fears and to settle for less than God intended. So, for your daughters' sake, don't lose your courage. And, if you have lost it, ask God to renew it.

PRAYER: Lord, where I am weak in courage, strengthen me. And I pray for my sister and friend who may be entrapped by the stronghold of fear, that she would walk in the liberty wherewith you have set her free. In Jesus' name. AMEN!

AFFIRMATION: I will live an abundant life through Christ Jesus. I have the courage to win. (repeat 3 times)

DAY 10

"I'M NOT ALRIGHT, BUT I WILL BE"

> *"Why art thou cast down, O my soul? And why art thou disquieted in me? Hope thou in God: for I shall yet praise Him for the help of His countenance."* Psalms 42:5
>
> *Why are you depressed, O my soul? Why are you upset? Wait for God! For I will again give thanks to my God for His saving intervention.* Psalms 42:5 (NET)

Believe it or not, precious woman of God, it is alright to not be alright sometimes. It is in those "not alright" moments where you learn to trust God more and depend on Him completely. It's in those moments where He becomes Jehovah Jireh, your provider, and Jehovah Rapha, your healer.

I can recall a time in life when I struggled with my emotions, and made life decisions based on where I was at the moment, not on where I was headed. I made permanent choices based on temporary problems or issues, because, in that moment, I was CONVINCED that it was the right thing to do.

My dear lady, may I suggest to you to stay clear of emotional, impulsive decisions because they can and will come back to haunt you. You may even feel justified in your actions, but if your decisions were fueled by a hot temper or mere frustration, it will bite you later and you could end up paying for it permanently. Here's the flipped side of the coin; you may be right in your decision but wrong in the timing of your execution of that decision, and you'll still end up paying for it.

Always remember, avoidance will never make an issue go away, neither will covering it with a church face because, at some point, it stops working. Oftentimes, the hardest face to face is your own, but you must look within yourself to find the Inner-Healing you need. And, the help that you need to deal with your real is in the presence of the Lord.

In today's Scripture reference, David has a void within himself; he has become downcast, meaning he's depressed, feeling low and dispirited, and he is disquieted, or feeling uneasy, full of anxiety, unnerved and disconnected. But, he stops to deal with what ails him. He talks to his own soul:

Soul, why are you disquieted? Why are you in despair? Why are you restless and disturbed? O, my inner self, why are you cast down; why are you dejected? Why are you in such turmoil and depressed? Why are you discouraged and sad? Soul, why have you been stuck here for so long, and, why can't you get over this?

David tells himself to "hope thou in God", which means trust God. *Trust in the Lord with all thine heart and lean not to thine own understanding. In all thy ways, acknowledge Him and He shall direct thy paths. Commit thy ways unto the Lord; trust also in Him; and he shall bring it to pass. Thou wilt keep him in perfect peace, whose mind is stayed on thee: because he trusts in thee.*

God is the only one who can change anything and everything about you and/or your circumstance. So, you must determine within yourself, that you will trust Him with everything you have, and that you'll praise Him while you're waiting for the manifestation of the end result. So, even if you're not alright right now, praise Him because you know you will be!

PRAYER: Father, I thank you that I am an overcomer, and, regardless to how I feel today, I decree and declare that You are freeing me from unnecessary anxieties and depressions because I trust in You. I know that the work You began in me will be completed, so I praise you in advance. In Jesus' name. AMEN!

AFFIRMATION: Today, I overcome myself; I walk in praise, not pressure, and, I believe in the God that believes in me. I release what I cannot change to Jesus Christ, and I cast all my cares upon Him. (repeat 3 times)

DAY 11

"FROM DESOLATION TO RESTORATION"

When I passed by you and saw you squirming in your blood, I said to you while you were in your blood, 'Live!' Yes, I said to you while you were in your blood, 'Live!' Ezekiel 16:6

If you're reading this book, then you're amongst the many that has experienced pain, disappointment, frustration, sorrow, grief, loneliness, anxiety, distress, defeat and anguish. These unfortunate circumstances of life will often leave you in a state of desperation and isolation; they will leave you broken and bleeding. Blood is an indication of an injury or a wound, and blood loss can be external or internal. Sometimes the wound is so deep until the bleeding is not easily stopped and, if you're not careful, your blood will spill onto others.

Now, once the wound begins to heal, a scar is created, and it reminds us that an injury has been sustained or a surgery has been performed. Far too often, scars embarrass us because we only view them through the lens of negativity, but, a scar is the manifestation of the skin's healing process! As stated earlier in this book, a process is "a series of actions or steps taken in order to achieve a particular end" and the scar can deceive us into thinking that we are further along in the process then we really are. A few weeks after major surgery, you may look and even feel completely healed, but your doctor, who has trained eyes will say you need more time because you're still in the process.

Since scars are not beauty marks, and their appearance can cause us shame and humiliation, we try to hide them, treat them and sometimes act as if they don't exist. But, just like the doctor who has medically trained eyes, people that are spiritually minded can often see what you're trying to hide; sometimes it's revealed through your own actions, attitudes and moods.

Today, God wants you to know that He sees you! He has seen you from the beginning; the blood from your rough childhood; He sees the pain from the divorce, the humiliation from the rape, the heartbreak from the rejection, the suicide attempt. He sees the distress from the abuse and violations. He sees the trail of blood from your traumas and tragedies, and sees you squirming in your own blood, but He says to you today, as He said to Jerusalem in Ezekiel 16:6, "LIVE!" The thief, your adversary, the devil has come to steal, kill and destroy, but Jesus says unto you, I AM come that you might have life, and have it more abundantly. LIVE! It is in Him that we LIVE, move and have our being!! LIVE, because you don't have to die in what's causing you to bleed. Declare this over your life, Psalms 118:17 "*I shall not die, but live, and declare the works of the Lord*."

Consider this: If you don't deal with your demons, then your daughter will have to fight them, because she will only become what she's seen exemplified.

May the oil of the Lord be released upon this day, setting you free in every aspect of your being from the field of blood. He will not leave you stained in blood but will wash you from the very evidence of the destruction. By His supernatural power, He moves you from the place of desolation to restoration today!

PRAYER: Father, in Jesus' name, I call myself from the field of depression, oppression, disappointment, anxiety, rejection, abuse and brokenness. Not only do I call myself, but my family as well. In Jesus' name. AMEN!

AFFIRMATION: I am no longer lost in the field of life, dying from my situations or circumstances. Today I live for the rest of my life!!

Day 12

"HIS PEACE IS YOURS"

Peace I leave with you, my peace I give unto you: not as the world giveth, give I unto you. Let not your heart be troubled, neither let it be afraid. John 14:27

"Master, the tempest is raging!
The billows are tossing high!
The sky is o'ershadowed with blackness,
No shelter or help is nigh:
"Carest Thou not that we perish?"
How canst Thou lie asleep,
When each moment so madly is threat'ning
A grave in the angry deep?
The winds and the waves shall obey Thy will.
Peace, be still! Peace, be still!
Peace, be still! Peace, be still!
Whether the wrath of the storm-tossed sea,
Or demons, or men, or whatever it be,
No water can swallow the ship where lies
the Master of ocean and earth and skies;

They all shall sweetly obey Thy will!
Peace! Peace! be still!
Whenever the Lord says "Peace", there will be
peace!
(*Author: Mary Ann Baker, written in 1874 – Public
Domain*)

How do you define peace? That question has been asked countless times and several responses have been given. Here are a few:

- a state of tranquility or quiet
- freedom from civil disturbance
- a state of security or order within a community provided for by law or custom
- freedom from disquieting or oppressive thoughts or emotions
- a lack of conflict and freedom from fear of violence between heterogeneous social groups. (Wikepedia.com)

The Old Testament Hebrew word for peace is *shalom*, referring to relationships between people, nations and God with men. Peace is a commodity that cannot be purchased with money because, ultimately, it is a gift from God. The New Testament Greek word for peace is *eirene*, referring to rest and tranquility. In a world filled with chaos and confusion, what we need more than anything else is peace, and, the peace of God provides a calm retreat during life's most difficult storms.

It's much easier to prepare for a storm when you've been warned of its approaching. Meteorologists have been trained to watch for impending storms, whether they be hurricanes, tornados, snow, hail, earthquakes or tsunamis. Warnings are sent out and watches are set so that the residents can be prepared. Preparation gives you a sense of peace that even if your lights and water are off and stores are closed, you'll still be able to manage because you have survival tools in place. But, sometimes, no matter how prepared you are, one storm can totally wipe out everything you've taken years to build. It's in those times where you need the peace that surpasses all understanding; the peace that will keep your heart and your mind. That is the peace that only Christ can give.

The storms listed above are obvious storms, some of them are seasonal, and others are predictable. But there are storms of life that are not so obvious, they're less visible and can also be silent: storms of divorce, disease or death; storms of betrayal, bankruptcy or blindness; storms of abuse, adultery or addiction; storms that leave lives shattered, hearts broken and hopes shredded; storms that turn dreams into nightmares. In these times of desperation and despair we must execute our right to run to the Rock of our salvation, knowing that He is our refuge and strength, and a very present help in trouble (Psalms 46:1). It is in His presence where there is fullness of joy and at His right hand there are pleasures forevermore (Psalms 16:11).

The promises of God are yea and Amen, and He promises, according to Jeremiah 33:6, to bring health and healing, and reveal an abundance of peace and truth to you today.

Proverbs 14:30 (NIV) says "*A heart at peace gives life to the body.*" And, when our ways please God, He makes even our enemies be at peace with us. (Proverbs 16:7)

Regardless to what howling winds and waves are blowing in your life right now, with your own mouth, declare and decree, as Jesus did, "Peace, be still!" Receive His peace today, not as the world gives because then it will only be temporal; but make His peace a permanent resident in your life. It's yours for the asking.

Now may the Lord of peace Himself continually grant you peace in every circumstance. 2 Thessalonians 3:16 (NASB)

PRAYER: Lord, I know it is your desire that I live in peace, so, I pray that You will help me not to worry about things I cannot change. Worry leads to fearfulness which leads to desperation. Give me the power to not allow past, present or future situations to disturb my peace. Help me to rest in Your peace. In the powerful name of Jesus. AMEN!

AFFIRMATION: Today, I am the recipient of emotional, mental, physical peace and healing in abundance. I live in the peace Jesus left for me when He ascended on high.

DAY 13

"YOU ARE IN THE ENTRANCE OF YOUR RECOVERY"

> *When Jesus saw him lie, and knew that he had been now a long time in that case, he saith unto him, Wilt thou be made whole?* John 5:6

Have you ever felt you've been in one place too long? Stuck? Trapped? Circling the same mountain repeatedly? Now, take a moment and ask yourself why. Why am I still here? Have I become content with where I am? How many more years will I stay in this position?

Today, I'd like to remind you that God has provided you a way out, and there is recovery for you. 1 Corinthians 10:13 (GNT) *"Every test that you have experienced is the kind that normally comes to people. But God keeps his promise, and he will not allow you to be tested beyond your power to remain firm; at the time you are put to the test, he will give you the strength to endure it, and so provide you with a way out."*

I, like many of you, have been guilty of holding on, for dear life, to things and, more specifically, people that I knew were not good for me. However, my need for companionship caused me to succumb and submit to what was bringing me harm. When my first love and I parted ways, I was bitter, broken and stripped, and though I knew I needed to let go, something made me keep trying even to my own detriment. What makes us hold onto unhealthy, unwholesome, toxic relationships? The answer: Soul ties!

What are soul ties? A soul tie is an emotional bond or connection that unites you with someone else. You can become bound to a person through your soul. Soul ties are formed through close friendships, through vows, commitments and promises, and through physical intimacy. Not all soul ties are bad. Genesis 2:24 - *Therefore shall a man leave his father and his mother, and shall cleave unto his wife: and they shall be one flesh.* And, 1 Samuel 18:1 - *And it came to pass, when he had made an end of speaking unto Saul, that the soul of Jonathan was knit with the soul of David, and Jonathan loved him as his own soul.*

But then there are soul ties that are formed outside the bond of marriage. 1 Corinthians 6:16 (CEB), "*Don't you know that anyone who is joined to someone who is sleeping around is one body with that person? The scripture says, 'The two will become one flesh'.*" This ungodly soul tie will cause a woman who is being treated like dirt to stay with the one who is misusing and abusing her. Whenever you commit fornication, a transfer of spirits take place and, although you know a relationship is not healthy, you'll keep going back. It's as if you can't help yourself, so, you need the power of God to break the chains of bondage off your neck.

Soul ties are strongholds, and they will dominate your life if not torn down. Strongholds are based on lies and deception, and they will cause your thinking to not be in alignment with the perfect will of God for your life. And if your thinking is defective or faulty or not aligned with God's will for you, you'll find yourself settling for less than the best He has for you.

2 Corinthians 10:4-5 says "*For the weapons of our warfare are not carnal, but mighty through God to the pulling down of strongholds; Casting down imaginations, and every high thing that exalteth itself against the knowledge of God, and bringing into captivity every thought to the obedience of Christ.*"

Since strongholds are based on lies, you must dispel them with truth. Jesus said, "*I AM the way, the truth and the life.* He also said in John 8:31-32 "*If ye continue in my word, then are ye my disciples indeed; And ye shall know the truth, and the truth shall make you free.*" Your knowledge of the truth will dismiss and dismantle every lie that the devil, the father of lies, presents to you. And because the power of life and death is in your tongue, when you speak truth, you're calling those things that be not as though they were.

Our scriptural reference today is from John 5 where a man who had an infirmity for 38 years sat by the pool of Bethesda where an angel would come down at a certain season and stir the water. Whoever got into the pool first, after the water was stirred, was healed of whatever infirmity he had. One day Jesus came along, saw the man, and knew how long he'd been in that case (how long he'd been infirmed, how long he'd been stuck, how long he'd been trapped, how long he'd been sitting, how long he'd been waiting) and he asked him one question: *Wilt thou be made whole*? In other words, you're right here at the entry of your deliverance, but you need to open your mouth and say what it is you want!

Are you at the verge of answered prayer, on the edge of a breakthrough but can't seem to break loose?

The man at the pool said, "*Sir, I have no man, when the water is troubled, to put me into the pool: but while I am coming, another steppeth down before me.*" He had believed the lie of the deceiver that the only way he could get healed was through human effort, but, because no one helped him, he remained in that condition. And, each time someone else was healed, he was distracted from his own healing!

Friend, you've been sitting by this pool too long. Make up your mind......no more distractions; I want to be made whole, so I release what's been holding me down and I'm walking into my destiny. I will no longer depend on the natural arms of man but on the supernatural power of God!

PRAYER: Lord give me the courage to pick myself up and walk away from the stuff that's holding me back. Break every stronghold, and may every root of bitterness be destroyed. I want to move from here and walk in my true destiny. Help me Lord; in Jesus' name. AMEN!

AFFIRMATION: Today I will do whatever it takes to move toward a better me. I will trust God to untie me from my past. I will be released from every stronghold and soul tie. (repeat 3 times)

DAY 14

"RELIEF COMES WITH YOUR RELEASE"

> *Come unto me, all ye that labour and are heavy laden, and I will give you rest.* Matthew 11:28

RELIEF: alleviation, ease, or deliverance through the removal of pain, distress, oppression, anxiety, depression.

RELEASE: to dismiss, freedom from confinement, bondage, obligation, pain, restraints, liberation from emotional strain.

Charles A. Tindley wrote a hymn in 1916 titled "Leave It There" and the lyrics are:

If the world from you withhold of its silver and its gold,
And you have to get along with meager fare,
Just remember, in His Word, how He feeds the little bird—
Take your burden to the Lord and leave it there.

If your body suffers pain and your health you can't regain,
And your soul is almost sinking in despair,
Jesus knows the pain you feel, He can save and He can heal—
Take your burden to the Lord and leave it there.

When your enemies assail and your heart begins to fail,
Don't forget that God in Heaven answers prayer;
He will make a way for you and will lead you safely through—
Take your burden to the Lord and leave it there.

When your youthful days are gone and old age is stealing on,
And your body bends beneath the weight of care;
He will never leave you then, He'll go with you to the end—
Take your burden to the Lord and leave it there.

Leave it there, leave it there,
Take your burden to the Lord and leave it there;
If you trust and never doubt, He will surely bring you out—
Take your burden to the Lord and leave it there.

(Public Domain)

There is relief in knowing you can release your burdens and cares into the Lord's hands because He can handle it no matter how great or small. We often become discouraged and bogged down in life's cares; its burdens are difficult to bear. Like Jesus, we are acquainted with grief and sorrow; mental and physical fatigue every so often overwhelms us because we desperately try to work out every problem in our own strength. This leads to weariness and exhaustion, but, the Word of God is our consolation.

The Bible declares in 1 Peter 5:7 *"Casting all of your care upon Him; for He careth for you."* And, Psalms 55:22 (AMP) *"Cast your burden on the Lord [release it] and He will sustain and uphold you; He will never allow the righteous to be shaken (slip, fall, fail)."* HE CARETH FOR YOU! HE WILL SUSTAIN YOU! HE WILL UPHOLD YOU! Allow these words to settle in your spirit! This gives us confidence and assurance and, like Paul, in 2 Corinthians 4:8-9, we can go ahead and declare our victory! YES, *" We are troubled on every side, YET not distressed; we are perplexed, BUT not in despair; Persecuted, BUT not forsaken; cast down, BUT not destroyed!!* The word "but" in this instance is used as a conjunction, joining two contrasting ideas. For instance, Joseph said to his brothers, in Genesis 50:20 *"ye thought evil against me; BUT God meant it unto good."*

Whatever you do in this season of your life, don't lose your "but"!

I'm hurting in my body BUT, by His stripes I'm healed.

I don't have the money right now BUT my God shall supply all my needs according to His riches in glory.

The enemy is coming against me BUT the Lord will fight for me; all I need to do is stand still and see the salvation of the Lord with me.

My patience is getting very low BUT if I wait on the Lord and be of good courage, He shall strengthen my heart.

I feel like I'm drowning in this sea of life BUT the Lord promised that when I pass through the waters, He will be with thee; and through the rivers, they shall not overflow me: when I walk through the fire, I will not be burned; neither shall the flame kindle upon me.

Yes, the weapon formed BUT it will not prosper.

Today, I speak rest, relief and release into you. And, I declare the same word that was given to the people of God in Isaiah 14:3-4 (AMP) "*And it will be in the day **when** the Lord gives you rest from your pain and turmoil and from the harsh service in which you have been enslaved, that you will take up this taunt against the king of Babylon (or whatever has oppressed you), and say, "How the oppressor has ceased, and how the fury has ceased!"*

Jeremiah 31:25 (NET) "*I will fully satisfy the needs of those who are weary and fully refresh the souls of those who are faint.*"

Psalms 37:7 *"Rest in the Lord, and wait patiently for him: fret not thyself because of him who prospereth in his way, because of the man who bringeth wicked devices to pass."*

Jesus beckons you to Himself; He is the only one who can provide exactly what you need. *Come unto me, all ye that labour and are heavy laden, and I will give you rest.* Take your burdens to the Lord and leave them there, because, your relief comes when you're willing to release everything you're holding onto into the hands of the Lord.

PRAYER: Father, it is my time for relief, so, I'm asking that you release me now and let me find rest in you. In Jesus' name. AMEN!

AFFIRMATION: I will rest before the Lord. Rest and peace comes to my mind, body and spirit. (repeat 3 times)

DAY 15

"ANXIETY CANNOT RULE"

> *Be anxious for nothing, but in everything by prayer and supplication with thanksgiving let your requests be made known to God. And the peace of God, which surpasses all comprehension, will guard your hearts and your minds in Christ Jesus.* (Philippians 4:6-7 NASB)
>
> *Commit thy way unto the Lord; trust also in him; and he shall bring it to pass. Psalms 37:5*
>
> *Commit your future to the Lord! Trust in him, and he will act on your behalf. Psalms 37:5(NET)*

According to American Psychological Association (APA), "**Anxiety** is an emotion characterized by feelings of tension, worried thoughts and physical changes like increased blood pressure. People with anxiety disorders usually have recurring intrusive thoughts or concerns."

Anxiety, a crippling disease, distracts us from our relationship with God and the truth that He is "Lord of heaven and earth"; it takes over our minds and plunges our thoughts into darkness. There are causes and triggers of anxiety, and we must be aware of both. Causes of anxiety can be your upbringing or genetics, but triggers are issues that make anxiety worse or prevalent, such as a stressful job or living with a disease, and even relational or social problems. Being overly concerned with family problems, troublesome children, church responsibilities and/or hurts can trigger anxiety.

In 1965, Evangelist Billy Graham wrote these words: ***Anxiety is the natural result when our hopes are centered in anything short of God and His will for us.***

It is not God's will that our lives are filled with fear, worry and anxiety, therefore, His Word constantly reminds us to:

Cast your burden on the Lord, and he will sustain you; he will never permit the righteous to be moved. Psalm 55:22 ESV

Casting all your anxieties on him, because he cares for you. 1 Peter 5:7 ESV

Fear not, for I am with you; be not dismayed, for I am your God; I will strengthen you, I will help you, I will uphold you with my righteous right hand. Isaiah 41:10 ESV

Come to me, all who labor and are heavy laden, and I will give you rest. Matthew 11:28 ESV

As we learn to trust in the Lord, anxiety's stronghold is broken. Trusting Him takes practice, so when negative circumstances arise, we should view them as opportunities to practice trusting God; opportunities to build our faith; opportunities to mature!

Several years ago, I had a heart attack, 100% of my main artery was blocked and it took almost a year to recover. It seemed my life was almost over; but thank God, almost isn't good enough. I was carrying undo anxiety and stress from worrying about things I had no control over. My son, whom I'd raised in the church, had become very rebellious and wanted nothing to do with me; he chose to hang with the wrong crowd and got in trouble in school; as we know, evil communication corrupts good manners. The enemy wanted to destroy his life! I prayed, fasted, counseled, and did everything I knew to do, yet there was no change. How can the preacher pull everyone out of the fire except her own son? He went from youth detention, to youth boot camp, to jail and finally to prison.

The stress was overwhelming to the point where I wanted to put down my own Bible, because it seemed to be working for others, but not me. I finally reached the point of realizing that I needed to shift my energy from stressing to trusting. I knew that, regardless of what the enemy was saying, my work was not over and I had a Kingdom assignment to fulfill.

So, I began to cast my trouble upon the only One who was able to handle it; my Savior, my God, my

King, my deliverer, my Comforter and He completely turned my son around. Today, not only is he a free man, but he's a great preacher, Pastor, father and a mentor to other young men. Don't give up on you children although they sometimes break your heart and disappoint you after you've invested so much in them; yet, there are lessons to be learned through their dilemmas. Take comfort in the fact that God has your child in His hands. Keep praying and trusting, and watch God turn them around.

You see, my trouble shoved me into the face of the Almighty God, it pushed me into a deeper relationship; it caused me to pray without ceasing because I refused to see my son die in the streets; it caused me to call on Him, knowing that He would answer and show me great and mighty things.

I decided that anxiety could not rule my life, because that would mean that it would have to sit on the throne of my heart, and there is only room for one KING on the throne, and that is Jesus Christ, the only begotten Son of God. And He reigns forever!

Speak to whatever stress or anxiety that's been trying to dominate you and let it know that there's NO ROOM IN THIS INN!

And they that know thy name will put their trust in thee: for thou, Lord, hast not forsaken them that seek thee. Psalm 9:10

PRAYER: Father, I thank you that anxiety does not have rule, dominion, or free reign in my life but You are the ultimate authority. Teach me to trust you more, in Jesus' name. AMEN!

AFFIRMATION: Today I will praise and not panic; I will be still and know that He is God; and I will believe God, knowing that He will bring it to pass.

DAY 16

"A JOURNEY TO WHOLENESS"

For I will restore health unto thee, and I will heal thee of thy wounds, saith the Lord; because they called thee an Outcast, saying, This is Zion, whom no man seeketh after. Jeremiah 30:17

Oxford Dictionaries define **journey** as an act of traveling from one place to another, and, a long and often difficult process of personal change and development.

Spiritual journey is a phrase used by many different religions to mean the natural progression of a person as they grow in understanding of God, the world, and himself. It is an intentional lifestyle of growing deeper in knowledge and wisdom.

The journey to wholeness can only be appreciated when you're coming from a place of brokenness. We can look at brokenness in several different ways. As it relates to humanity and God, we all came into this life broken. From the first day that we entered this world, we were in a broken relationship.

Something that is broken is reduced to fragments, damaged, destroyed, crippled, hurt, injured, shattered, shredded, smashed. And because of Adam's sin, our relationship with our heavenly Father was broken. But thank God for the shed blood of Jesus Christ because He paid a price that we couldn't pay; He fulfilled a debt that He did not owe. The Bible says in *2 Cor. 5:21 that "He made Him to be sin for us, who knew no sin; that we might be made the righteousness of God."* So, the work of the cross was Jesus making a way for man not to live in a broken state all his life.

Now, as it relates to our spiritual lives, we can choose whether we want to remain broken or be made whole; to accept or not accept Christ; to live or not live for Him.

As we look at brokenness from the aspect of life and the issues of life, to be broken is to be down-hearted, downtrodden, oppressed, depressed, wearied, weighed down, burdened, heavy hearted or dis-hearted, physically, mentally, financially, emotionally exhausted or drained, beaten, burnt out, cried out, given out.

Life and its circumstances and situations have a way of breaking us down, but, one thing we women have learned, or are in the process of learning, is the art of covering it up. We feel it necessary, imperative or needful to cover our wounds or bruises. WHY? Perhaps because of positions and titles, or, we don't want to be considered weak.

Many times, when we see trouble approaching the first thing we do is ask God to take it away or take us out of it. But, God doesn't want to TAKE YOU OUT, He wants to TAKE YOU THROUGH!

Your testimony is so much more effective when you've gone through, when you've not given up, when you've not thrown in the towel or let anyone else throw in the towel on you; when you've held on, when you've learned to praise with tears locking under your chin; when you've persevered even when you didn't know how it was going to work out.

We are like CLAY in the hands of the POTTER, and the clay dare not say to the potter "what are you doing" or "what are you making". When a vessel is being made for use, it has to be molded and pressed and beaten and stretched and then put into abnormal heat. When it is ready to come out of the heat, the potter listens for a sound and when it hears a particular sound he brings it out because he knows it is now ready to be used.

The vessel that is made is not made for its own use; it's made for the use of someone else. 2 Timothy 2:20-21 states *"But in a great house there are not only vessels of gold and of silver, but also of wood and of earth; and some to honor, and some to dishonor. If a man therefore purge himself from these, he shall be a vessel unto honor, sanctified, and **meet for the master's use**, and prepared unto every good work."*

People, by their comments, opinions, taunts, insults, criticisms, abuse and disrespect have a way of breaking you down, and ofttimes, you can find no one with the right words to bring you back to wholeness. The psalmist said in Psalms 69:20 *"Reproach or insults have broken my heart and I'm full of heaviness and I looked for someone to take pity but there was no one; I looked for comfort but I found none."* But that is when you have to look to the hills from whence cometh your help, knowing that all of your help comes from the Lord.

Whether you're broken because you lost a loved one, or a friend betrayed you, or you lost a job, or your daughter got pregnant, or your son is on drugs, or you went through a divorce or your finances are all messed up, God wants you to look to Him so you will know, that you know, that you know that He alone is the One who heals the brokenhearted and He alone binds up their wounds.

The journey to wholeness takes time, patience, prayer and perseverance. Yes, it would be great if we could blink an eye and everything completely changed for the good, but that's not reality; it is a process and process takes time. So, take one day at a time, allow God to walk you through each step of this journey and seek to gain wisdom and insight from each situation. We've all made bad choices and judgments, and we've all experienced taking the wrong path, but the great news is, when you realize you've made a wrong turn, a bad choice, a terrible move, all you must do is reroute.

Most of us have a global positioning system (GPS) in our cars that we use to take us from one destination to the next. Ofttimes, because we feel we know the way, a better way, or a shortcut, we will ignore the instructions of the GPS only to find ourselves lost. But the system lives up to its name, and to position us properly onto the path of our destination, it reroutes us. It is the same with the Holy Spirit; He leads and guides us into all truth, and whenever necessary, to keep us on track to our divine destiny, He will reroute us.

God has promised to restore your health and heal your wounds. Rest in His promises.

PRAYER: Lord, as I journey toward wholeness, strengthen my faith in You; help Thou mine unbelief, let me trust You, knowing that each step is ordered by You. In Jesus' name. AMEN!

AFFIRMATION: I'm more than a conqueror and I can do all things through Christ who strengthens me. I am not a victim, but a victor. I will be made whole and complete, mind, body and spirit.

DAY 17

"BREAK THE CYCLE AND MOVE FORWARD"

Only take heed to thyself, and keep thy soul diligently, lest thou forget the things which thine eyes have seen, and lest they depart from thy heart all the days of thy life: but teach them thy sons, and thy sons' sons. Deuteronomy 4:9

Then we turned, and took our journey into the wilderness by the way of the Red sea, as the Lord spake unto me: and we compassed mount Seir many days. And the Lord spake unto me, saying, Ye have compassed this mountain long enough: turn you northward. Deuteronomy 2:1-3

The Israelites were considered to be "children of the COVENANT" which is an agreement between two people or two groups that involves promises on part of each to the other. Biblically speaking, a covenant is not like a contract that has an expiration date but it is a permanent agreement. The Bible lets us know that Abraham obeyed the voice of the Lord, and kept

His charge, His commandments, His statutes, and His laws. And, because of his obedience, his seed was blessed! (What you do now will affect your children later.) God said, *I will make thy seed to multiply as the stars of heaven, and will give unto thy seed all these countries; and in thy seed shall all the nations of the earth be blessed*. Genesis 26:4

But here are some things we need to consider:

The Israelites spent 40 years on a journey that should have taken 11 days. *When you know God has promised you something and it seems to take forever to come to pass, check to see if the problem lies within you.*

It was not the distance that kept them from reaching their promise, but it was the condition of their hearts. God didn't want to take them into a new land with an old <u>heart</u>.

The wilderness was to prepare them to live in obedience once they arrived in their new place.

God used the wilderness experience to break them and to humble them because they had become stiff-necked and hard-hearted, and arrogant. So, the wilderness was necessary in their preparation of obtaining what God had promised.

The wilderness taught them that God was their <u>provider</u>!

The Israelites murmured and complained against Moses saying, "*You brought us into this wilderness to die of hunger.*" In other words, they said, at least when we were in Egypt we had food to eat; we had more than enough and we didn't have to worry about anything!

So, God said to Moses, I'm going to provide for them, but I'm going to give them just enough bread for the day. The Lord had to cause the Israelites to remember all the ways which He had led them in the wilderness for forty years, and He said I did this *"to humble thee, and to prove thee, to know what was in thine heart, whether thou wouldest keep MY commandments, or no."*

*"And he humbled thee, and suffered thee to hunger, and fed thee with manna, which thou knewest not, neither did thy fathers know; **that he might make thee know that man doth not live by bread only, but by every word that proceedeth out of the mouth of the Lord** doth man live. Thy raiment waxed not old upon thee, neither did thy foot swell, these forty years."* Deuteronomy 8:3

Simply put, what the Lord was teaching the children of Israel is the same lesson He's teaching us today: DON'T FORGET TO REMEMBER the ways that I've made, the mercies that I've shown, the times I've rescued you. DON'T FORGET TO REMEMBER my faithfulness granted you on a day to day basis. DON'T FORGET TO REMEMBER that I rebuked the Red Sea, stood the water up like a wall, and dried the ground so that you could walk across safely! DON'T FORGET

TO REMEMBER that I, the Lord, saved you and redeemed you from the hand of the enemy! DON'T FORGET TO REMEMBER that when the enemy came in like a flood, I, the Lord your God, lifted up a standard against him.

The Israelites committed so many sins and trespasses against the Lord; they served or went whoring after other gods, they sacrificed their children unto devils, they shed innocent blood. Yet, time after time he delivered them because He is a God of covenant.

You have compassed the mountain of crying, complaining, murmuring, doubting; the mountain of unbelief, regression, feeling inadequate and insufficient; the mountain of lack, pain, hate, failure, procrastination, abuse and misery long enough. Break the cycle, the course or series of events or operations that have been recurring regularly and leading you back to your starting point, and move forward. Forget those things which are behind and press on!!

PRAYER: My Father God, I ask nothing from You today, instead, I want to say thank you for being a covenant keeping God. In Jesus' name. AMEN!

AFFIRMATION: My God makes all things new, and I will follow Him forward.

DAY 18

"THIS IS YOUR APPOINTED TIME"

And he was teaching in one of the synagogues on the sabbath. And, behold, there was a woman which had a spirit of infirmity eighteen years, and was bowed together, and could in no wise lift up herself. And when Jesus saw her, he called her to him, and said unto her, Woman, thou art loosed from thine infirmity. And he laid his hands on her: and immediately she was made straight, and glorified God. Luke 13:10-13

There is a time and a season for all things; a time for things to begin and a time for them to end. Nothing remains the same. We have all experienced times in our lives where we've wondered; will this ever end? Will my circumstances change? Will I get better or is this my forever? When will this pain go away? When will my tears stop flowing? When will it be my turn?

Lashawn Pace wrote a song several years ago that echoes the sentiments of David in Psalms 31:15a "*My times are in thy hand.*" Some of the lyrics to her song are:

> *If I were in control of my life*
> *I think that I would have worked things out*
> *differently;*
> *There would be no hurt,*
> *no pain, no disappointments;*
> *of these things my life would be scott free,*
> *But that just goes to show, how little I know*
> *about leading,*
> *about controlling my life;*
> *For you see all these things*
> *have worked together just to make the best of me.*

Human nature causes us to want to govern and control every situation and circumstance in our lives, but we must realize that God sets the seasons, and if He sets them, He's in control of them. God will deliberately take control out of your hand so that when the problem is solved, the issue is no longer, the pain is gone, the tears have faded, the hurt has disappeared, the prayer is answered, He ALONE will get the glory! Don't be weary in your well doing, because you have a DUE SEASON coming if you don't faint!

The infirmed woman in our referenced Scripture, was bowed or bent over for 18 years; that's someone's lifetime, and she could in "*no wise*" lift up herself. She was in a situation wherein she could not help herself. Regardless to how much she tried to unbend, straighten the situation, fix the problem, she was helpless to do so. However, Jesus met her in the synagogue; in other words, she kept coming to church! Too often, when we are going though rough seasons, we will isolate ourselves, we forsake our assembling together, we cut off all fellowship from the people of God, but, that's when the enemy will wear us down and wear us out. Daniel 7:25 talks of a beast that will arise, "*And he shall speak great words against the Most High, and shall wear out the saints of the most High*". Our adversary, the devil, seeks to devour the people of God, but our advocate, our helper and our defender, Jesus Christ, intercedes on our behalf and always causes us to triumph.

You, like this infirmed woman, may have suffered for years, but, as there was an appointed time set for her, there is an appointed time set for you. When God says enough is enough, it simply means your appointed time has come.

Jesus called this woman to Himself, spoke to her and said "*Woman, thou art loosed from thine infirmities*" and immediately, what kept her bowed, bent over, and bound for 18 years had to loosen its grip or stronghold off her. Loosed means to be set free from, no longer fastened or attached to something or someone. It took belief, faith, and trust in the power of God to cause this woman to leave her seat and position herself in front of Jesus. I'm sure during the course of the 18 years, she'd seen Him work miracles in the lives of others and had to fight with the doubt that He'd ever do it for her. But she arose, and came to Jesus just like she was, and that step of faith caused her to walk into her season of healing. ONE WORD loosed her forever, never to be bound by "that" thing again.

Whatever "that" thing is that has had you bound, stuck, in a stupor for years, today, hear the Word of the Lord, woman, THOU ART LOOSED FROM THINE INFIRMITIES.

I believe that this is your appointed time and God is moving on your behalf, however, it is imperative that you too believe, and don't allow doubt and unbelief to steal what rightfully belongs to you.

For as he thinketh in his heart, so is he. Proverbs 23:7

Jesus healed this woman publicly so that all who knew her, had ridiculed her, had humiliated her, and had counted her out, would see the evidence of her healing and would have to testify that God is able to do all things but fail.

God is doing the same for you today; receive it by faith and get ready to experience your own "immediately"!

PRAYER: Father, God, I thank you for setting me free from years of bondage. I receive it in Jesus' name. AMEN!

AFFIRMATION: I am loosed today, not based on my feelings, but on my faith!

DAY 19

<u>"LET IT GO AND BE FREE!"</u>

> *Watch out that no poisonous root of bitterness grows up to trouble you, corrupting many.* Hebrews 12:15b (NLT)
>
> *So the two of them continued on their journey. When they came to Bethlehem, the entire town was stirred by their arrival. "Is it really Naomi?' the women asked. 'Don't call me Naomi,' she told them. 'Instead, call me Mara, [meaning bitter] for the Almighty has made life very bitter for me. I went away full, but the LORD has brought me home empty. Why should you call me Naomi when the LORD has caused me to suffer and the Almighty has sent such tragedy?' Ruth 1:19-21* (NLT)

Do you find yourself constantly rehearsing, rehashing or replaying incidences, conversations or other happenings in your life that have brought you to a point of bitterness? Are your thoughts constantly fixated on a person whose done you wrong? Have you justified your anger or frustration toward him, her, or them, and, is it fulfilling to you to withhold forgiveness? Then, my friend, on this 19th day of Inner-Healing for your soul, it is important that we expose the **root of bitterness.**

Bitterness is unresolved, unforgiven anger and resentment, especially when you feel you've been treated unfairly. It is something that is germinating or constantly growing beneath the surface of your persona and, like a root, it digs deep into the soil of your heart. Bitterness is characterized by an unforgiving spirit and a negative or critical attitude.

Bitterness hardens your heart on the inside and disfigures your countenance on the outside. Not only does it defile you, but, because bitterness is contagious, it also defiles those around you. Our referenced Scripture says, *"Watch out that no poisonous root of bitterness grows up to trouble you,* ***corrupting many"****; (the KJV says, "lest any root of bitterness springing up trouble you, and* ***thereby many be defiled****.")* The poisonous root of bitterness can infect your marriage, children, friends, church and even your community. The more you dwell on what has been done to you, the injustice you have suffered, or the loss you've incurred, the deeper the root of bitterness grows.

Bitterness spreads like weeds, and every good gardener knows you can't just chop weeds down; they must be pulled up by the roots. If not, they'll continue coming back, and they don't come alone; they bring more weeds with them.

Ephesians 4:31(NASB) says, *"Let all bitterness AND wrath AND anger AND clamor AND slander be put away from you, ALONG WITH all malice."*

Watch this progression: Bitterness, left unchecked or undealt with, leads to extreme anger (which is wrath), which will lead to clamor (or demanding what you want.) And, when that proves unfruitful, you begin to slander or talk bad about the person you're bitter towards, to get others to agree with you. Finally, because the root has been left unchecked and has dug deep into your heart, it will cause you to want to bring harm to the person you're bitter towards.

As Christians, or believers, God wants to reveal to you the contents of your own heart. In order to experience the healing that God has for you, there must be a willingness on your part to forsake the sin of bitterness. Sure, it may seem easier and even justifiable to hold onto it, but, the Word of God, which we use to govern our lives says, *"Get rid of all bitterness, rage, anger, harsh words, and slander, as well as all types of malicious behavior. And be kind to one another, tenderhearted, forgiving one another, **even as** God in Christ forgave you.* Ephesians 4:31-32 (NLT).

It's not easy to forgive but it's necessary, even when our flesh says, "But I've been unjustly wronged". To be unforgiving hurts no one but you. The person you're angry with and bitter towards has gone on with his or her life, and you are left with the root. Throughout Scripture, we are reminded of our duty to forgive: Colossians 3:12-13 (NLT), *"Since God chose you to be the holy people whom he loves, you must clothe yourselves with tenderhearted mercy, kindness, humility, gentleness, and patience. You must make allowance for each other's faults and forgive the person who offends you. Remember, the Lord forgave you, so you must forgive others."*

And the Word of God also says, *"For if ye forgive men their trespasses, your heavenly Father will also forgive you: But if ye forgive not men their trespasses, neither will your Father forgive your trespasses."* (Matthew 6:14-15).

This will require you to say as David did in Psalm 139:23-24 (NLT), *"Search me, O God, and know my heart; test me and know my thoughts. Point out anything in me that offends you, and lead me along the path of everlasting life."*

Ofttimes, our bitterness, like Naomi in our above referenced Scripture, is toward God because we feel He treated us unjustly by taking something or someone from us; or by not allowing things to work out as **we planned.** My friend, God is sovereign; He reigns over the entire universe; He can do whatever He wants, whenever He wants, however He wants, and He never makes mistakes. Now, since He is a good Father who is perfect in all His ways, and has declared, *"For, as the heavens are higher than the earth, so are my ways higher than your ways, and my thoughts than your thoughts",* we must trust that fact that He will work all things out for our good because we love Him.

Had Naomi's daughter-in-law, Ruth, never lost her first husband, she would not have been in position to meet Boaz, and they would never have given birth to Obed, the father of Jesse, the father of David through whose lineage came Jesus Christ.

You may not understand why God has allowed you to through the things you've gone through, lose the things you've lost, suffer the things you've suffered, or cry the tears you've cried, but know this, He's unfolding His divine plan for your life. Jeremiah 29:11, *"For I know the thoughts that I think toward you, saith the Lord, thoughts of peace, and not of evil, to give you an expected end."* Let go of all bitterness, anger, hatred, unwillingness to forgive, and whatever else you've been holding onto; let it go so that you can be free!

PRAYER: Father, I confess my sin of bitterness, and thank you for revealing and exposing the root of bitterness in my heart. Now, Father, I ask for your help to uproot every area of bitterness in my heart and life, and, even in places where I'm unaware the root has grown, reveal it so that it can be removed. Forgive me for infecting anyone with the bitterness of my own heart, and now, my Father, let Your love abound. In Jesus' name. Amen!

AFFIRMATION: I Am Free!!

DAY 20

"TODAY I CHOOSE TO WORSHIP"

> *Thine, O Lord is the greatness, and the power, and the glory, and the victory, and the majesty: for all that is in the heaven and in the earth is thine; thine is the kingdom, O Lord, and thou art exalted as head above all.* 1 Chron. 29:11

Much of our time thus far has been spent reminiscing on the circumstances of our lives, but, on this 20th day of Inner-Healing, let us focus our attention solely on God, and let Him be the object of our affection. Isaiah 26:3 says, *"Thou wilt keep him in perfect peace, whose mind is stayed on thee: because he trusteth in thee."*

Worship denotes worthiness, and the only One who is worthy of all praise, honor, glory and adoration is God and God alone.

My Father, I come to You today with gratefulness in my heart; worshipping You for who You are. You said of Yourself, "I am God and beside me there is none other. I will be exalted amongst the nations; I will be exalted in the earth. Be still and know that I am God; I will be exalted among the heathen. There's nobody like Me. To whom will you liken Me, or make Me equal or compare Me?"

You, oh Lord, are the one who brought me out of darkness, into the marvelous light. You are the one who heals me emotionally, physically, spiritually, psychologically. You are the one who delivered me and established my goings. You, oh God, have sanctified me and justified me. You stand alone! You spoke and it was, it is, and it will always be! This entire world is upheld by the word of Your power! There will never be a time when You are not, because You always was, always are, and will always be. You are the alpha and the omega; the first, last and everything in-between. Everything was created by You and for You!

Oh God, I choose to worship You because You are above all things, through all things and in all things! Before You there was no God formed, neither will there be after You!

You are omnipresent; everywhere at one time! You are omniscient, knowing everything; before there is a thought formed, oh God, You know it! You are omnipotent – all powerful, almighty, all sufficient, unstoppable. You are sovereign; reigning over everything – the heavens, the earth, the seas and everything within. Absolutely all power is in Your hand to do whatever You want, whenever You want, and use whomever You want to use. YOU ARE GOD!!

You are great and greatly to be praised. You are to be feared above all gods. The glory belongs to You! The majesty belongs to You! The power belongs to You! The victory belongs to You! Dominion belongs to You! You are high and lifted up! You are exalted above all others!

You're a covenant keeping God! Your loving-kindness and tender mercies endure forever! Your law is perfect! Your testimony is sure! Your statutes are right! Your commandments are pure! Your judgments are true and righteous!

Every knee must bow to you, and every tongue will confess that You are Lord. Every nation will know that You are God because You will prove yourself Holy in their sight.

It is Your mighty hand and Your outstretched arm that gives me victory! Oh God, I choose to worship you! The earth is Yours, the fullness thereof, the world and they that dwell therein. You alone do great wonders! Your counsel is great! Your deeds are mighty! Your eyes are always upon Your children and Your ears are opened to their cries. You are excellent, marvelous, incredible, amazing, wonderful! You are the God of all flesh and there is nothing too difficult for You! Your wonders never cease; Your compassions never fail! Oh God, I choose to worship!

You lift up the downcast and downtrodden; You mend the brokenhearted and heal all wounds. I bless and honor You, my Father. You are highly exalted.

You have put gladness in my heart, a song on my lips, laughter in my mouth, joy in my soul, and peace in my inner man. You have turned my mourning into joy, given me beauty for ashes and replaced my spirit of heaviness with a garment of praise!! Oh, my Father, God, I will bless You at all times and Your praise shall continually be in my mouth.

My Father, I choose to worship You and thank You for my Inner-Healing!

DAY 21

"IN CONCLUSION"

Finally, brethren, whatsoever things are true, whatsoever things are honest, whatsoever things are just, whatsoever things are pure, whatsoever things are lovely, whatsoever things are of good report; if there be any virtue, and if there be any praise, think on these things. Philippians 4:8

Day 1 – God is reliable, unfailing and can be trusted. No matter what you face, God's greatness will strengthen you for the task.

Day 2 - Never run away when you don't feel the strength to endure. Stand still and trust God with all your heart, and don't lean to your own understanding. God is not a man that He should lie, therefore, He will bring you through whatever storm you face because He has promised to never leave nor forsake you.

Day 3 - Our obstacles may seem insurmountable, overwhelming, impossible and impassable, yet, if we are steadfast, unmovable and always abounding in the work of the Lord, victory will be our portion. If we are spiritually grounded and not driven and tossed by the winds of life, we will triumph over every situation and in every circumstance.

Day 4 - The storm is in His hand; the extent of the storm is in His hand; He created the storm therefore he can demand it to cease when it has served its purpose. HE STILL STILLS STORMS!

Day 5 - We must not focus on what we can see, but on what we cannot see, for, what we can see is temporal, but what we cannot see is eternal!

Day 6 - Who you are is who are, and, all you can do is all you can do. Don't live your life trying to make an impression on others because, at the end of the day, you'll be the only one struggling to figure out how to get out of what you've gotten yourself into.

Day 7 - Pick yourself up out of this place of defeat and press into your place of victory! No, it won't be easy, but it will be worth it! Desperation always brings restoration!

Day 8 - God wants to heal your every hurt and disappointment; He wants to take away all your guilt and shame, your oppression and depression. You may be able to hide your wounds from others, but the all-seeing eye of God knows exactly where you're hurting the most and He is the Balm of Gilead, ready and willing to bring you to complete healing, restoration and wholeness.

Day 9 - Fear and the loss of courage will cause you to be held captive in relationships that are not healthy. Courage is what you need to take control of your life.

Day 10 - Oftentimes, the hardest face to face is your own, but you must look within yourself to find the Inner-Healing you need. And, the help that you need to deal with your real is in the presence of the Lord.

Day 11 - Consider this: If you don't deal with your demons, then your daughter will have to fight them, because she will only become what she's seen exemplified.

Day 12 - Regardless to what howling winds and waves are blowing in your life right now, with your own mouth, declare and decree, as Jesus did, "Peace, be still!" Receive His peace today!

Day 13 - Friend, you've been sitting by this pool too long. Make up your mind......no more distractions; I want to be made whole, so I release what's been holding me down and I'm walking into my destiny.

Day 14 - Whatever you do in this season of your life, don't lose your "but"!

Day 15 - As we learn to trust in the Lord, anxiety's stronghold is broken. Trusting Him takes practice, so when negative circumstances arise, we should view them as opportunities to practice trusting God;

opportunities to build our faith; opportunities to mature!

Day 16 - Many times, when we see trouble approaching the first thing we do is ask God to take it away or take us out of it. But, God doesn't want to TAKE YOU OUT, He wants to TAKE YOU THROUGH!

Day 17 - You have compassed the mountain of crying, complaining, murmuring, doubting; the mountain of unbelief, regression, feeling inadequate and insufficient; the mountain of lack, pain, hate, failure, procrastination, abuse and misery long enough. Break the cycle and move forward.

Day 18 - Whatever "that" thing is that has had you bound, stuck, in a stupor for years, today, hear the Word of the Lord, woman, THOU ART LOOSED FROM THINE INFIRMITIES.

Day 19 - It's not easy to forgive but it's necessary, even when our flesh says, "But I've been unjustly wronged". To hold onto unforgiveness hurts no one but you. The person you're angry with and bitter towards has gone on with his or her life, and you are left with the root of bitterness. Let it go, and be free!

Day 20 – Focus on God; let Him be the object of your affection. Choose to worship, not worry.

Day 21 – The conclusion of the whole matter is this: whatever things are true, honest, just, pure, lovely and of a good report, purposely, think on these things.

GLOSSARY

Anger – a strong feeling of hostility or displeasure.

Anxiety – feeling overwhelmed or stressed by life, an apprehensive uneasiness or nervousness over an impending or anticipated ill.

Attitude – a mental position with regard to a fact or state; a negative or hostile state of mind.

Bitterness – deep anger for being treated unfairly; caused by or expressive of severe pain, grief or regret.

Compulsive – lack of control, not able to resist your urges or desires.

Cynical – a lack of trust for others, doubtful or suspicious of everyone.

Depression - feelings of severe despondency and dejection.

Discouragement – to feel disheartened, crushed, disappointed.

Fearful – feeling afraid or horrified by something, someone or of something happening.

Guilty – a feeling of responsibility or remorse for some offense.

Hate – an intense hostility and aversion usually deriving from fear, anger or sense of injury.

Hostility – aggressive behavior toward a person or thing, having animosity.

Hurt – physical and mental pain and injury.

Loneliness – to feel alone or unwanted, the feeling of emptiness, bleakness or desolation.

Low self-esteem – low worth towards self; feeling unworthy, incapable and incompetent.

Pessimistic - pertaining to or characterized by pessimism or the tendency to expect only bad outcomes; gloomy; joyless; unhopeful.

Resentment - the feeling of displeasure or indignation at some act, remark, person, etc., regarded as causing injury or insult.

Restless – impatient, difficult to be still, feeling unsettled, nervous or worried.

Sadness – gloomy, emotional pain, despondency.

Shame – a painful emotion caused by consciousness of guilt, shortcoming, or impropriety.

Unforgiving – unwilling or unable to forgive.

ABOUT THE AUTHOR

Dr. Bonnie B. Hill was saved in 1977 and started the ministry of Inner-Healing in 1995. For many years now, she has traveled throughout the country as an Evangelist, preaching the gospel of Jesus Christ and changing the lives of countless men and women.

She is the wife of Clemmie Hill for 40 years, the mother of 5, the nana of 10 and the great-nana of one.

Born and raised a PK (preacher's kid) to the parents of the late Elder John Robinson, Jr. and Mother Maxine Robinson.

The Inner-Healing ministry was birthed out of her own pain as a Christian, and, because of her transparency, many people have been restored.

She has spent her life's journey helping others to find a place of healing because she believes God wants us all to be healed and made whole.

The ministry of Dr. Bonnie Hill is based off St. Luke 4:18 *"The Spirit of the Lord is upon me, because he hath anointed me to preach the gospel to the poor; he hath sent me to heal the brokenhearted, to preach deliverance to the captives, and recovering of sight to the blind, to set at liberty them that are bruised."*

<u>DAILY NOTES</u>

1:_____

_____

_____

2:_____

_____

_____

3:_____

_____

_____

4:_____

_____

_____

5:_____

_____

_____

6:_____

_____

_____

7:_____

_____

_____

DAILY NOTES

8:_____

_____

_____

9:_____

_____

_____

10:_____

_____

_____

11:_____

_____

_____

12:_____

_____

_____

13:_____

_____

_____

14:_____

_____

_____

<u>DAILY NOTES</u>

15:_____

_____

_____

16:_____

_____

_____

17:_____

_____

_____

18:_____

_____

_____

19:_____

_____

_____

20:_____

_____

_____

21:_____

_____

_____

Made in the USA
Columbia, SC
02 March 2019